OTHER HELEN EXLEY GIFTBOOKS:
Garden Lovers Quotations
Rose Lovers Address Book

ÉDITED BY HELEN EXLEY
ILLUSTRATED BY JULIETTE CLARKE

Published simultaneously in 1999 by Exley Publications in Great
Britain, and Exley Publications LLC in the USA.
Copyright © Helen Exley 1999
The moral right of the author has been asserted.

12 11 10 9 8 7 6 5 4 3 2 1

ISBN 1-86187-121-X

A copy of the CIP data is available from the British Library. All rights
reserved. No part of this publication may be reproduced in any form.
Printed in China.
Exley Publications Ltd, 16 Chalk Hill, Watford, Herts WD1 4BN, UK.
Exley Publications LLC, 232 Madison Avenue, Suite 1409, NY 10016, USA

Acknowledgements: The publishers are grateful for permission to reproduce
copyright material. Whilst every reasonable effort has been made to trace copyright
holders, the publishers would be pleased to hear from any not here acknowledged.
Beverley Nichols: *From Down The Garden Path* published by Jonathan Cape Ltd

THE LITTLEST
Gardening
GIFTBOOK

◪ EXLEY
NEW YORK • WATFORD, UK

PARADISE

A garden is a little bit
of heaven on earth.

STUART AND LINDA MACFARLANE

What is paradise?
But a garden, an orchard of
trees and herbs full of pleasure
and nothing there but delights.

WILLIAM LAWSON

ALL MY HURTS
MY GARDEN SPADE
CAN HEAL.

RALPH WALDO EMERSON
(1803-1882)

I have never had
so many good ideas day after day
as when I work in the garden.

JOHN ERSKINE
(1509-1591)

THOUGHTS AND DREAMS

In my garden there is a large
place for sentiment. My garden
of flowers is also my garden
of thoughts and dreams.
The thoughts grow as freely
as the flowers,
and the dreams
are as beautiful.

ABRAM LINWOOD URBAN

INNER PEACE

Working in the garden... gives me
a profound feeling of inner peace.
Nothing here is in a hurry. There
is no rush toward accomplishment,
no blowing of trumpets. Here is
the great mystery of life and growth.
Everything is changing, growing,
aiming at something, but silently,
unboastfully, taking its time.

RUTH STOUT

THE GREATEST MIRACLE
OF ALL

There is nothing like a garden
for making you feel small.
There you are, right in the middle
of the greatest miracle of all —
the world of growing things.

GEOFF HAMILTON (1936-1996)

*Watching
something
grow
is good for
morale.
It helps you
believe in life.*

MYRON S.
KAUFMANN

GLOSSARY OF
GARDENING TERMS:

Annual: A plant that completes its life cycle in one season (the term season means between two and ten days).

Cloche: A small shelter for slugs, snails and woodlice.

Herbicide: An expensive method
of watering weeds.

Humus: A large pile created
from crops and plants that refused
to grow.

Perennial: Any plant that survives
for more than three months.

STUART AND LINDA MACFARLANE

What a man needs
in gardening
is a cast-iron back
with a hinge on it.

CHARLES DUDLEY WARNER
(1829-1900)

One of the most pleasing
sounds of Springtime,
to be heard all over
the country, is the contented
cooing of osteopaths
as Man picks up his
garden spade.

OLIVER PRITCHETT

So deeply is the gardener's instinct
implanted in my soul,
I really love the tools with which
I work — the iron fork, the spade,
the hoe, the rake, the trowel,
and the watering-pot are pleasant
objects in my eyes.

CELIA THAXTER
(1835-1894)

GARDENER'S LAWS:

(1) Other people's tools work only in other people's gardens.

(2) Fancy gadgets don't work.

(3) If nobody uses it, there's a reason.

(4) You get the most of what you need the least.

FROM "THE OFFICIAL RULES"

Falling trees gravitate towards greenhouses.

A friend has borrowed the tool you need most.

Nature prefers weeds.

The brightest apple contains the biggest worm.

A whirling lawn mower finds the lost gnome.

STUART AND LINDA MACFARLANE

A real gardener
is not a man who cultivates flowers;
he is a man who cultivates the soil....
If he came into the Garden of Eden
he would sniff excitedly and say:
"Good Lord, what humus!"

KAREL ČAPEK (1890-1938)

Ladies like gifts
of florist's flowers.
Lady gardeners
like a sack of
good manure.

PAM BROWN, b.1928

THE GREAT BORAGE WAR

How pretty, you say.
And for the next ten years
you are at war with borage.

PAM BROWN, b.1928

Gardeners work side by side
with nature. The gardener
struggles to raise some plants
while nature produces
an abundance of weeds.

STUART AND LINDA MACFARLANE

The fine old place
never looked more like a delightful
home than at the moment:
the great white lilies were in flower;
the nasturtiums, their pretty leaves
all silvered with dew, were running
away over the low stone wall;
the very noises around had a heart
of peace within them.

GEORGE ELIOT
(MARY ANN EVANS)
(1819-1880)

DAWN

It is good to be alone
in a garden at dawn or dark
so that all its shy presences
may haunt you
and possess you in a reverie
of suspended thought.

JAMES DOUGLAS

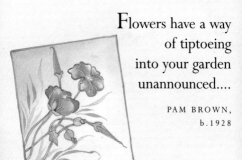

Flowers have a way
of tiptoeing
into your garden
unannounced....

PAM BROWN,
b. 1928

*Every morning the garden
presents you with a gift.
An astonishment.
The first white rose.
Sprig of green on the bush
you thought was dead.
Seeds sprouting.
A forgotten clump of violets.
A little joy.*

PAM BROWN, b.1928

To have a garden
is to live in a kaleidoscope
of light and shade,
of myriad leaves,
of breeze-touched blossom,
that changes
from minute to minute
and never remains the same.

PAM BROWN, b.1928

GARDENERS BOTH...

I watch through the window.
Grandad and grandchild in
the vegetable garden, working
their way down the rows.
Heads bent together, small
face peering, old hand pointing.
They straighten, nod their heads.

What are they discussing?

The ravages of cabbage whites?

The need to net the fruit?

The sturdiest way to fix the bean

poles? On they go. Sixty years

between them. Gardeners both.

PAM BROWN, b.1928

LOVE YOUR FLOWERS.
BY SOME SUBTLE SENSE
THE DEAR THINGS ALWAYS
DETECT THEIR FRIENDS,
AND FOR THEM
THEY WILL LIVE LONGER
AND BLOOM MORE FREELY
THAN THEY EVER WILL
FOR A STRANGER.

JULIA S. BERRALL

PEACE AND REST

IN THE ANCIENT WORLD
IT WAS EVER THE GREATEST
OF THE EMPERORS AND THE WISEST
OF THE PHILOSOPHERS
THAT SOUGHT PEACE AND REST
IN A GARDEN.

SIR GEORGE SITWELL

Everything that slows us down
and forces patience,
everything that sets us back
into the slow cycles of nature,
is a help.
Gardening is an instrument
of grace.

MAY SARTON

Real beauty is neither
in garden nor landscape,
but in the relation of both
to the individual, that what
we are seeing is not only
a scenic setting, but a
background for life.

SIR GEORGE SITWELL

THE ROSES!

And the roses – the roses! Rising out of the grass, tangled round the sun-dial, wreathing the tree-trunks, and hanging from their branches, climbing up the walls and spreading over them with long garlands falling in cascades –

they came alive day by day, hour by
hour. Fair, fresh leaves, and buds —
and buds — tiny at first, but swelling
and working Magic until they burst
and uncurled into cups of scent
delicately spilling themselves over
their brims and filling the garden air.

FRANCES HODGSON BURNETT (1849-1924)

Of all human activities,
apart from the procreation of children,
gardening is the most optimistic
and hopeful.
The gardener is by definition
one who plans for and believes
and trusts in a future,
whether in the short
or the longer term.

SUSAN HILL

THE REAL CREATORS

We little people, we who have
painted no masterpieces,
won no great prizes
– have yet created wonders.
From time and skill
and simple things,
we have made gardens.

PAM BROWN, b.1928

*I try to express
in physical form what I feel
on an inner level.
I think a garden should delight
the eye, warm the heart
and feed the soul.*

H.R.H.
THE PRINCE
OF WALES,
b.1948

EVERY FLOWER
ABOUT A HOUSE CERTIFIES
TO THE REFINEMENT
OF SOMEBODY.
EVERY VINE CLIMBING
AND BLOSSOMING
TELLS OF LOVE AND JOY.

ROBERT G. INGERSOLL
(1833-1899)

OBSESSION!

A garden is like those
pernicious machineries which
catch a man's coat-skirt or
his hand, and draw in his arm,
his leg, and his whole body
to irresistible destruction.

RALPH WALDO EMERSON
(1803–1882)

*Let no one think that real
gardening is a bucolic and
meditative occupation.
It is an insatiable passion,
like everything else to which
a man gives his heart.*

KAREL ČAPEK (1890-1938)

You Can't Let Go

Gardens... start with months
of sweat and toil, big ideas
and aching joints, excitements and
disappointments, successes and
failures, laughter and tears.
Until one fine day you realise
that you're hooked and your home plot
has become a part of you that you
simply can't let go.

GEOFF HAMILTON
(1936-1996)

SUMMER STORM

Gardeners never have to listen
to weather forecasts –
they know that as soon
as they start work in their garden
it will rain.

STUART AND LINDA MACFARLANE

As I write this, on June 29th,
it's time for another summer storm
to smash the garden to pieces,
though it may hold off until
the phlox, tomatoes, daylilies,
and zinnias are in full sway.

HENRY MITCHELL

*People from a planet
without flowers would think
we must be mad with joy
the whole time
to have such things about us*

IRIS MURDOCH
(1 9 1 9 - 1 9 9 9)

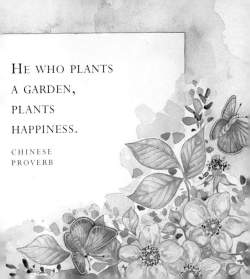

HE WHO PLANTS
A GARDEN,
PLANTS
HAPPINESS.

CHINESE
PROVERB

There is nothing so drab, so dead,
so spiky, sprawling, soggy, as a garden
in winter.
One drifts along the borders, disconsolate
One never can quite remember the
summer that is past. One never can quit
believe that it will ever come again.
So that every spring
is an astonishment
– a reawakening of joy.

PAM BROWN, b.192

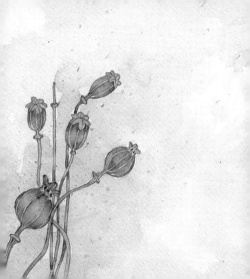

Our garden is now
a wilderness of sweets.
The violets, sweet briar,
and primroses perfume
the air, and the thrushes
are full of melody
and make our concert
complete.

MRS DELANY

The peace of the garden
descends upon me. The green
leaves enfold me.
Time, and the car, they are both
forgotten... and it is an agonizing
business, to say goodbye
to a garden. Often, when the car
has been panting outside

in the lane, I have run back
for one last look... there was
a lily I had forgotten...
or a bluebell that was almost
blue... or a rose that was
in hiding, among the quiet
shadows on the wall.

BEVERLEY NICHOLS

"But this rose is an extra"

All other things, our desires,
our food, are really necessary
for our existence in the first instance.
But this rose is an extra. Its smell
and its colour are an embellishment
of life, not a condition of it.

SIR ARTHUR CONAN DOYLE
(1859-1930)

OUR STRENGTH

Everybody needs beauty
as well as bread,
places to play in and pray in,
where Nature may heal
and cheer and give strength
to body and soul alike.

JOHN MUIR

A garden
is the microcosm
of our lives
– a constant changing,
a constant loss,
– a constant creation.
Always a new wonder.
Always a new hope.

PAM BROWN, b.1928

A LIFE OF DISASTERS

The "grass may be greener
on the other side of the fence"
but it grows twice as fast
on this side.

STUART AND LINDA
MACFARLANE

The kiss
of the wind for lumbago,
The stab of the thorn for mirth,
One is nearer to death
in the garden
Than anywhere else on earth.

ELEANOR PERENYI

IT'S SPRING TIME
IT'S WEED TIME

*To gardeners, onion grass
is a harbinger not of spring's delights
but of chickweed, bindweed, knotweed,
pigweed plantain, purslane and all
the other intruders that will spoil their
little Edens — nature's backhanded way,
gardeners feel, of making them pay
for some original horticultural sin.*

AUTHOR UNKNOWN

BUGS AND SLUGS RULE OK!

While gardeners strive
for the perfect rose,
aphids strive
for the perfect meal.

STUART AND LINDA MACFARLANE

On every stem, on every leaf...
and at the root of everything that grew,
was a professional specialist in the shape
of grub, caterpillar, aphids, or other
expert, whose business it was to devour
that particular part.

OLIVER WENDELL
HOLMES
(1809-1894)

FLOWERS
ARE LIKE THE PLEASURE
OF THE WORLD.

WILLIAM SHAKESPEARE
(1564-1616)

The Amen!
of nature is always a flower.

OLIVER WENDELL HOLMES
(1809-1894)

When at last I took the time
to look into the heart of a flower,
it opened up a whole new world
– a world where every country
walk would be an adventure,
where every garden would
become an enchanted one...
as if a window had been opened
to let in the sun.

PRINCESS GRACE OF MONACO
(1929-1982)

THERE IS A GARDEN
IN EVERY CHILDHOOD,
AN ENCHANTED PLACE
WHERE COLORS ARE BRIGHTER,
THE AIR SOFTER,
AND THE MORNING MORE FRAGRANT
THAN EVER AGAIN.

ELIZABETH LAWRENCE

HOPES

In all the recipes for happiness
I have ever seen, "something to
look forward to" has been given
as an important ingredient.
Something to look forward to!

How rich the
gardener, any
gardener, is in this
particular integrant!

For always he looks forward
to something if it is only
the appearance of red noses
of peonies in the spring or
the sharp aromas that fill the
air in autumn after the frost
has touched the herbage.

LOUISE BEEBE WILDER

*When I walk out of my house
into my garden
I walk out of my habitual self,
my everyday thoughts,
my customariness of joy and sorrow
by which I recognise and assure
myself of my own identity.
These I leave behind me
for a time, as the bather leaves
his garments on the beach.*

ALEXANDER SMITH (1830-1867)

ON A WARM SUMMER EVENING…

I can think of few diversions more soothing, more restful to the soul, than an hour spent [watering with a can], on a warm summer evening in an old country garden with a cat in attendance. The fragrance that rises from the grateful earth is like a benison; there is a subtle, shadowy beauty in the darkening soil, a ghostly music in the soft hiss and gurgle of the water.

BEVERLEY NICHOLS,
FROM "CATS A.B.C."

A gardener
is never shut out from his garden,
wherever he may be.
Its comfort never fails.
Though the city may close about him,
and the grime and soot descend
upon him, he can still wander
in his garden,
does he but close his eyes.

BEVERLEY NICHOLS

A GOOD DAY'S WORK

A gardener
stands and surveys a day's work.
The edging crisp,
the flopping plants invisibly staked.
The roses dead-headed,
the vine cut back.
And smiles.
And knows next week
it's all to do again.

PAM BROWN, b.1928

*On the first
warm day of spring
I dig my fingers deep
into the soft earth.
I can feel its energy,
and my spirits soar.*

HELEN HAYES
(1900-1993)

When there's new growth
bursting out all over, everything fresh,
green, and flourishing, the plants
are little rockets of success
going off....

JAQUELINE HERITEAU

Each spring... a gardening instinct,
sure as the sap rising in the trees,
stirs within us.

LEWIS GANNETT